INTRODUCTION

Words have power. *"The pen is mightier than the sword"* still rings true today. Words can change how we see the world and impact our actions. Whether written or spoken, words can evoke a full spectrum of emotions. Words can be serious, demonstrative, playful and, yes, even cringeworthy.

FORWARD

Welcome to a *"fun-sized"* book of cringeworthy words.
This book is the culmination of a 10-plus-year quest to collect
and showcase some of the most awkward and embarrassing
words in the English language. While the primary meaning of these
words may not make you think twice, over time they have taken
on alternative meanings that, well, may make you wince.
And, in many cases, it's not the meaning of the word, but
how it sounds when spoken causes you to squirm.

BOOK

of those words™

A "fun-sized" picture book
of cringeworthy words.

By Russ Napolitano

The concept for this book came about spontaneously during
an agency/client strategy planning session. All it took was the innocent
use of one word with the group reacting, *“That word makes me cringe”*
and we were off on a tangent. I would occasionally revisit this list, adding
to it as more people were eager to contribute. This list eventually grew
to well over 30 words, many of them seemingly innocent words that
morphed into double entendres, solidifying my original idea that
I had what I needed to publish my first ***Book of those words*™**.

Thanks to the advent of AI-generated artwork, my business
partner and Xhilarate’s lead creative, Michael McDonald, convinced
me that we could do this and have fun doing it. With the help of
Midjourney AI®, Michael created the supporting visuals and
ChatGPT® assisted me in giving each word its meaning.

"GET READY TO DIVE INTO THE COLORFUL,
CRINGE-WORTHY, AND CAPTIVATING WORLD
OF WORDS WITH EITHER SLANG OR
DOUBLE MEANINGS. BUCKLE UP AND BRACE
YOURSELF FOR THE UNEXPECTED TWISTS

FROTHY

This adjective can have several meanings: having a lot
of bubbles or foam, as in frothy coffee or a frothy drink. It's also
used to describe speech or writing that is trivial, superficial,
or lacking substance, as in *"frothy rhetoric."*

TESTY

An adjective that means irritable, touchy, or easily annoyed. For example, *"The customer became testy when the store was out of stock."* It is often used to describe someone who is short-tempered or quick to show anger.

03

SWALLOW

As a noun, it describes a type of songbird with a slender body and long, pointed wings. As a verb, it refers to the process of taking food, drink or something/someone into the body through the mouth and down the throat. A common phrase, *"hard to swallow,"* refers to something that's difficult to believe.

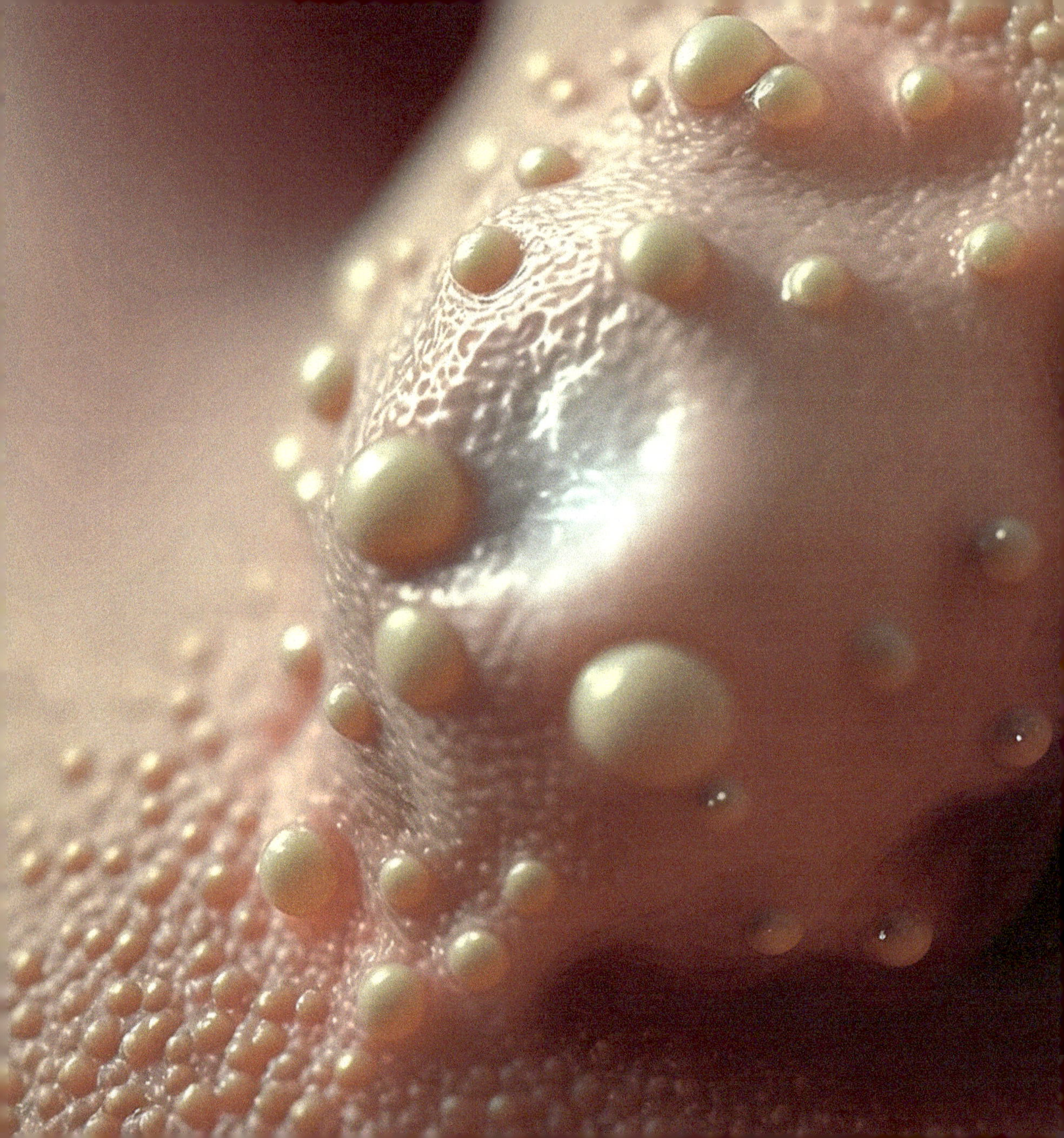

PUS

At the risk of TMI, *"pus"* refers to a thick yellowish or greenish fluid that forms at the site of an infection or wound in the body. It is a mixture of dead white blood cells, bacteria, and tissue debris. Our preoccupation with pus may explain the popularity of Dr. Pimple Popper.

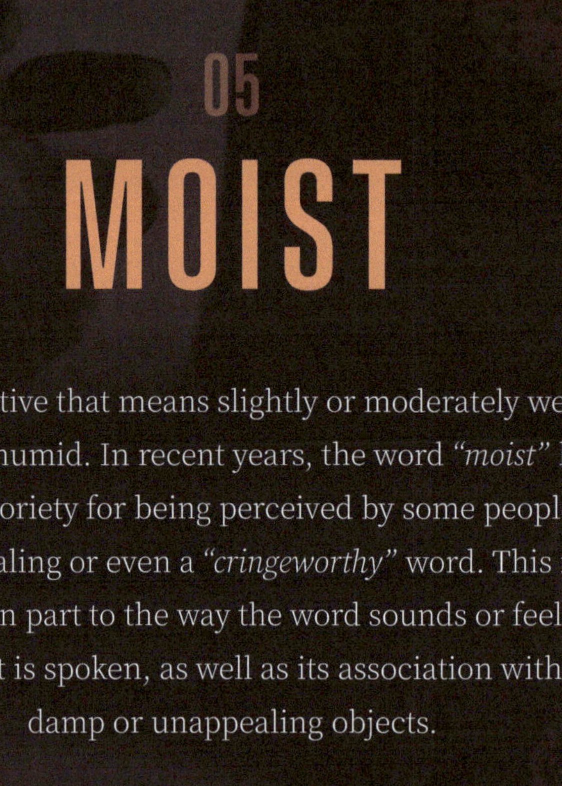

MOIST

An adjective that means slightly or moderately wet, damp, or humid. In recent years, the word *"moist"* has gained notoriety for being perceived by some people as an unappealing or even a *"cringeworthy"* word. This may be due in part to the way the word sounds or feels when it is spoken, as well as its association with damp or unappealing objects.

MOUNT

LOAD

As a noun, it refers to a quantity of something, especially a heavy quantity, as in *"a load of laundry."* As a verb, *"load"* means to put a quantity of something into a container, machine, or vehicle, as in *"to load a truck with boxes."* The word *"load"* can also be used as a slang term to refer to a bowel movement or to the contents of a soiled diaper. That's probably where we get the phrase *"a load of crap,"* referring to utter nonsense.

SEEPAGE

A noun that refers to the gradual and slow leakage of a liquid or gas, especially from a container or surface. For example, *"seepage of water from a damaged dam."* The word *"seepage"* can be used as a vulgar or crude term to refer to an embarrassing or unsanitary situation, such as a bodily fluid escaping from someone's clothing.

THROBBING

An adjective that describes a rhythmic beating or pulsing,
such as a heartbeat or a headache. For example,
"a throbbing headache or member."

PHLEGM

A noun that refers to a thick, sticky mucus produced in the throat and lungs, especially because of a cold or respiratory infection. For example, *"he coughed up phlegm."*

GIRTH

A noun that refers to the circumference of an object,
such as the waist or a tree trunk.

SNATCH

As a noun, it can refer to an act of snatching or quickly seizing something or it can refer to the external genital organs of a human being, especially of a woman.
As a verb, it can mean to grab or steal something quickly.

TOOL

A noun with several different meanings. It can refer to
an implement used for a particular purpose, such as a hammer
or a screwdriver. It can also refer to a device or piece of equipment
used to perform a task. *"Tool"* is also a slang term describing someone
who is being a jerk or acting in a foolish or annoying manner.
A common phrase, *"not the sharpest tool in the shed,"* refers
to someone who is lacking in intelligence.

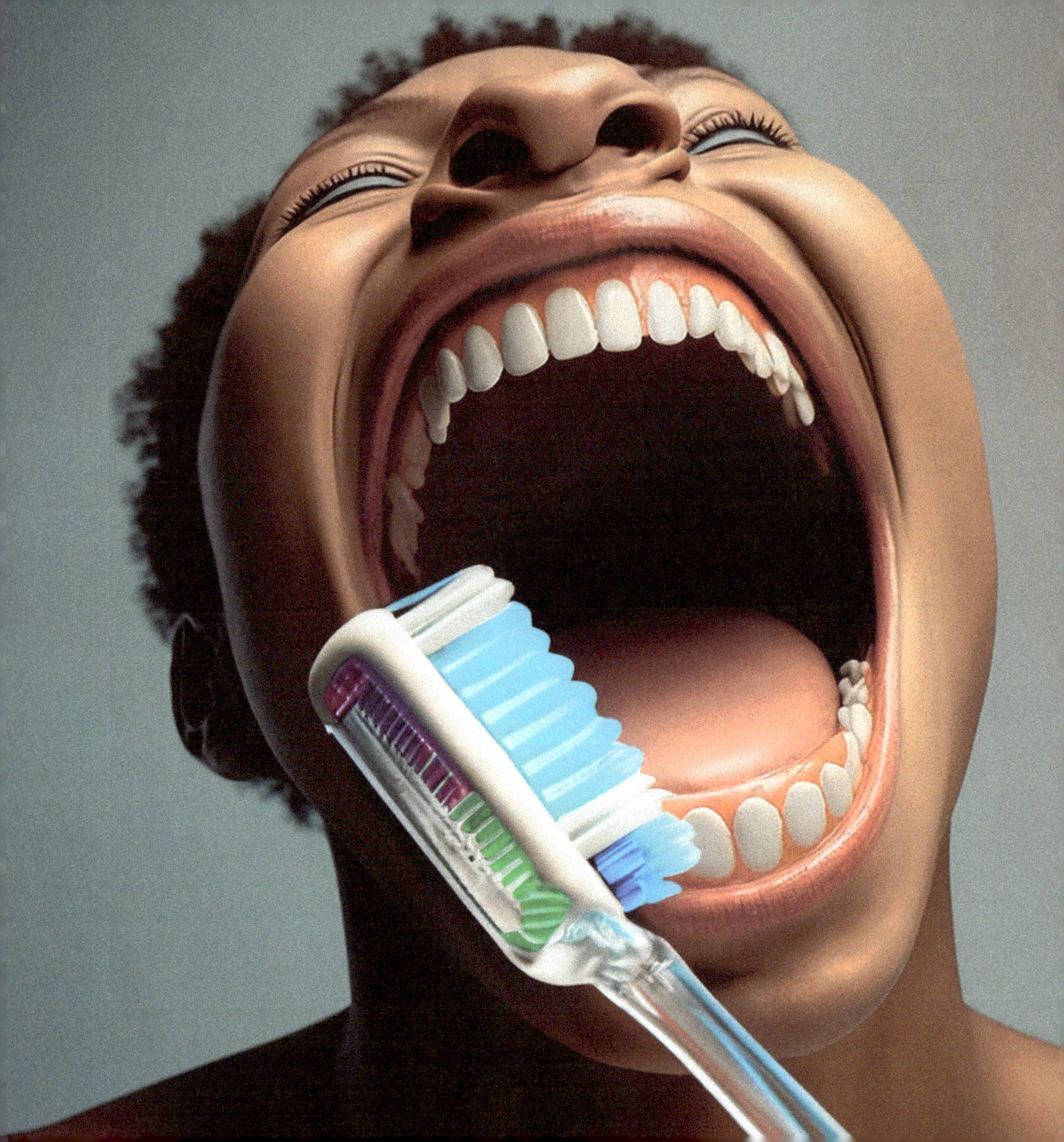

ORAL

As an adjective, it can be used to describe things relating to the mouth, such as oral hygiene or oral surgery. It can also be used to describe things that relate to speech, the act of speaking, or a type of sexual action involving the mouth.

SLIT

A noun that refers to a narrow cut or opening.
It can be used to describe a cut made in a piece of
material, such as fabric or paper.

FLACCID

An adjective that refers to a state of being limp,
relaxed, or not firm. It is commonly used to describe
body tissues, muscles, or organs that have lost
their normal tension and elasticity.

17

WIPE

A verb that means to clean or dry *(something)* with
a cloth, a piece of paper, or one's hand. It can also refer
to the act of removing or erasing something. Today, the word
also has become a noun, a disposable cloth relied upon
for diaper duty, removing stains from clothing, or
other even less glamorous uses.

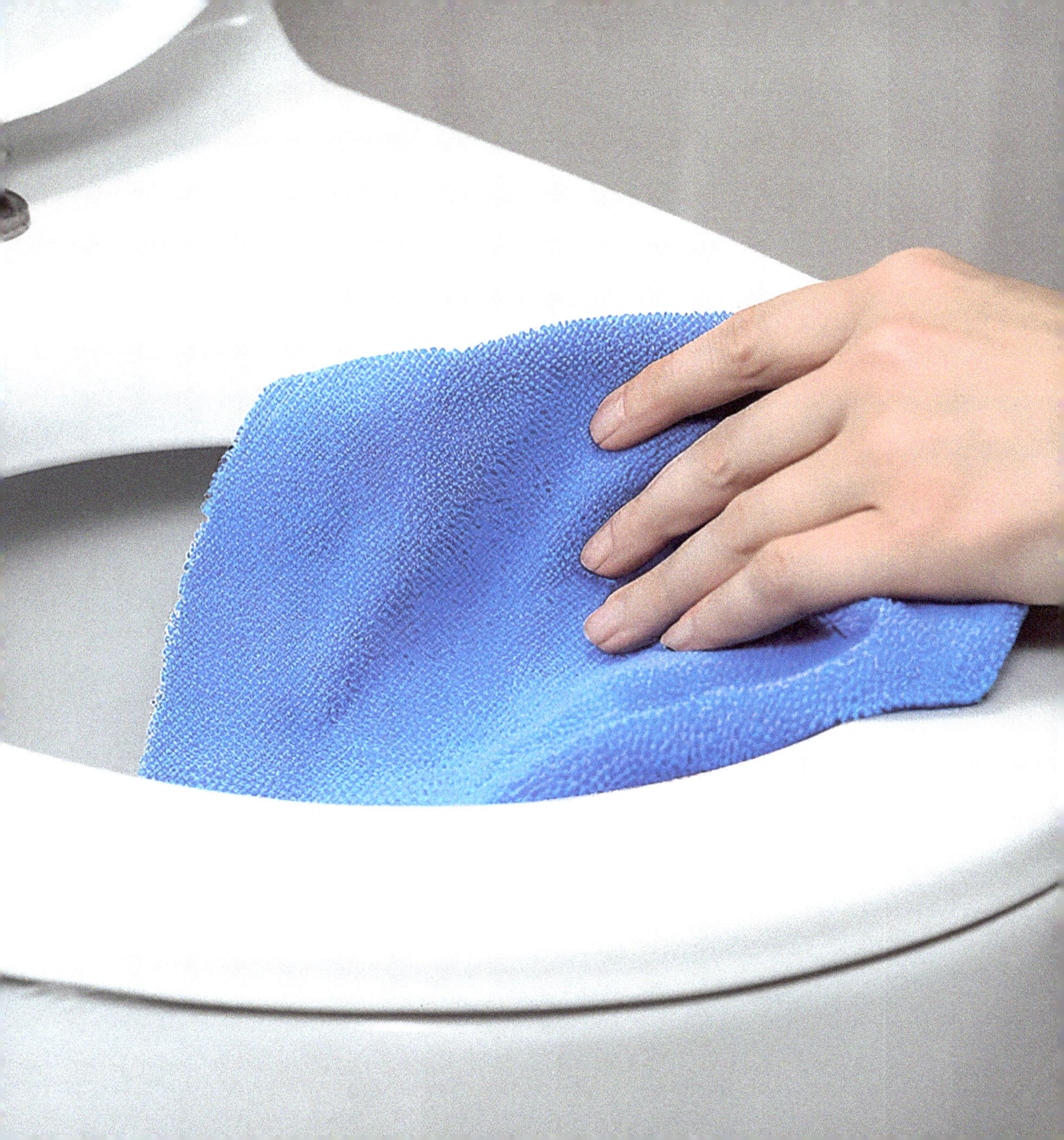

18

SPEW

A verb that means to forcefully eject or discharge something
(such as food, vomit, hateful rhetoric, or politicians' platitudes) from
the mouth. It can also be used to describe the emission of a
substance or material, such as lava from a volcano.

TOE JAM

This is definitely not something you want to spread on
your morning toast. It's a colloquial term that refers to a mixture
of dirt, sweat, and other debris that accumulates between the toes.
(Not to be confused with *"camel toe,"* another cringeworthy phrase
which, if you don't know what it means, we encourage you
to Google® it. And, yes, Google® is also a verb.)

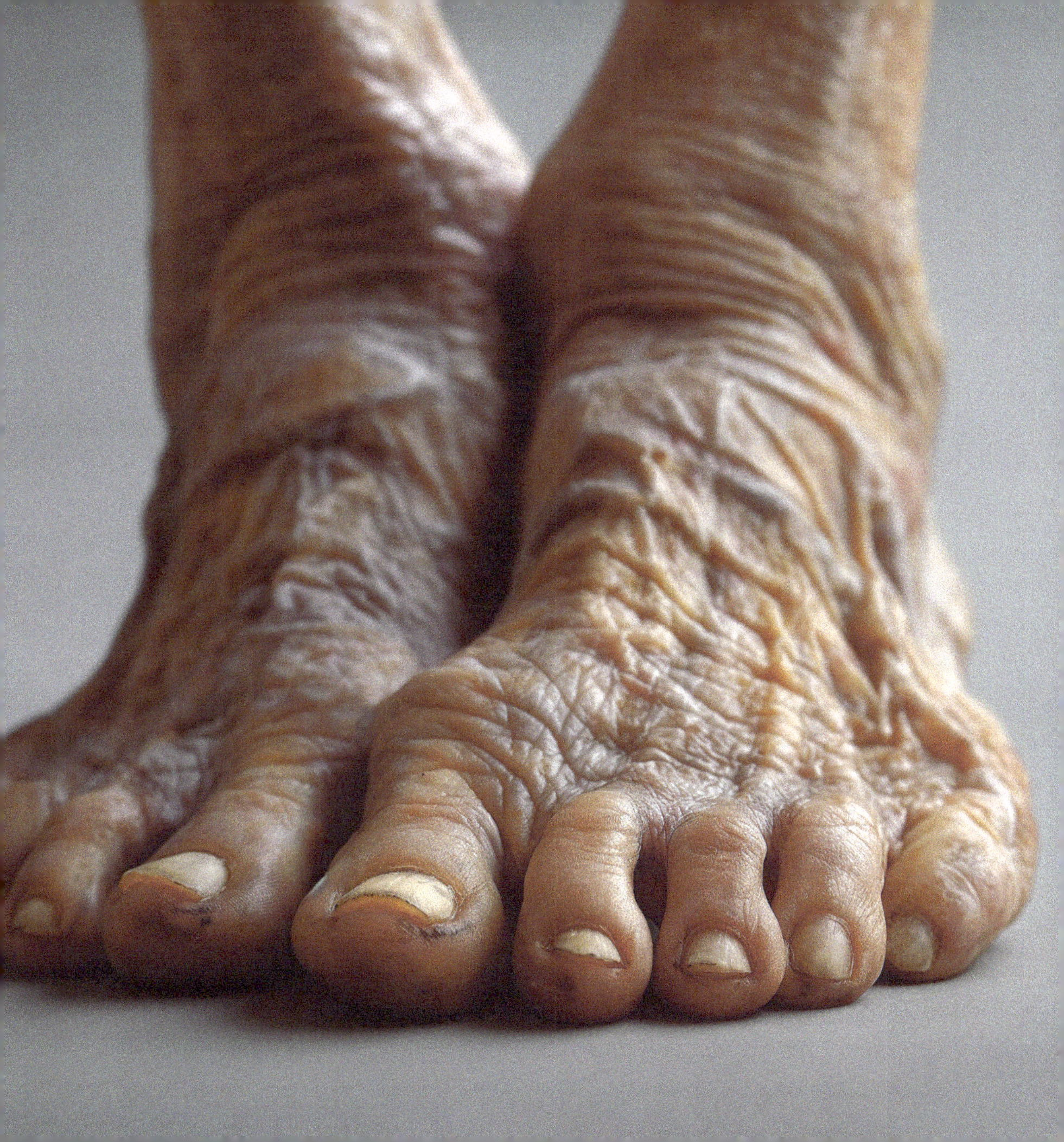

JUNK

Old or discarded articles that are considered useless or of little value. Over time, the word junk has become American English slang for a man's genitals. The phrase refers to the offense many people took to the November 2010 decision by TSA to begin full body pat downs of airline passengers in the U.S. who refused to go through a full body scanner.

EXTRACTION

This word may bring to mind the ominous sound of a dentist's drill. *"Extraction"* refers to the act of removing or taking something out. It can refer to a wide range of actions, including removing a tooth, extracting a sample of material, or extracting information from a data source.

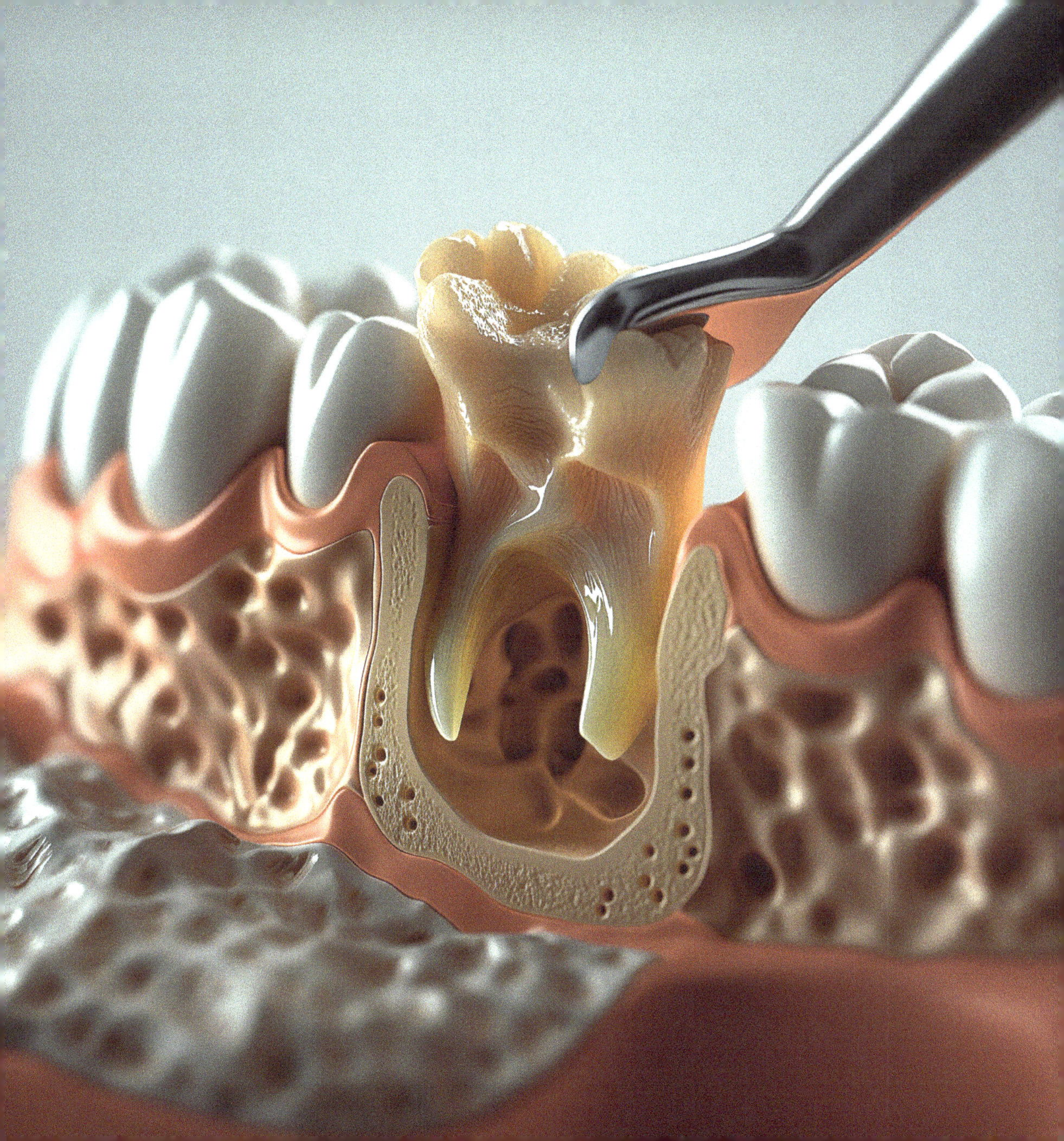

DUMP

A verb that means to throw away, get rid of, or unload.
It can also be a noun referring to a place where waste
or garbage is disposed of. *"Dump"* is also slang
for having a bowel movement.

23

SHAFT

A noun that means a long, cylindrical object, such
as a spindle or a tool handle. It's also an underground passage
for a mine, a lift, or an air shaft, or a lever that transmits
power or motion in a machine.

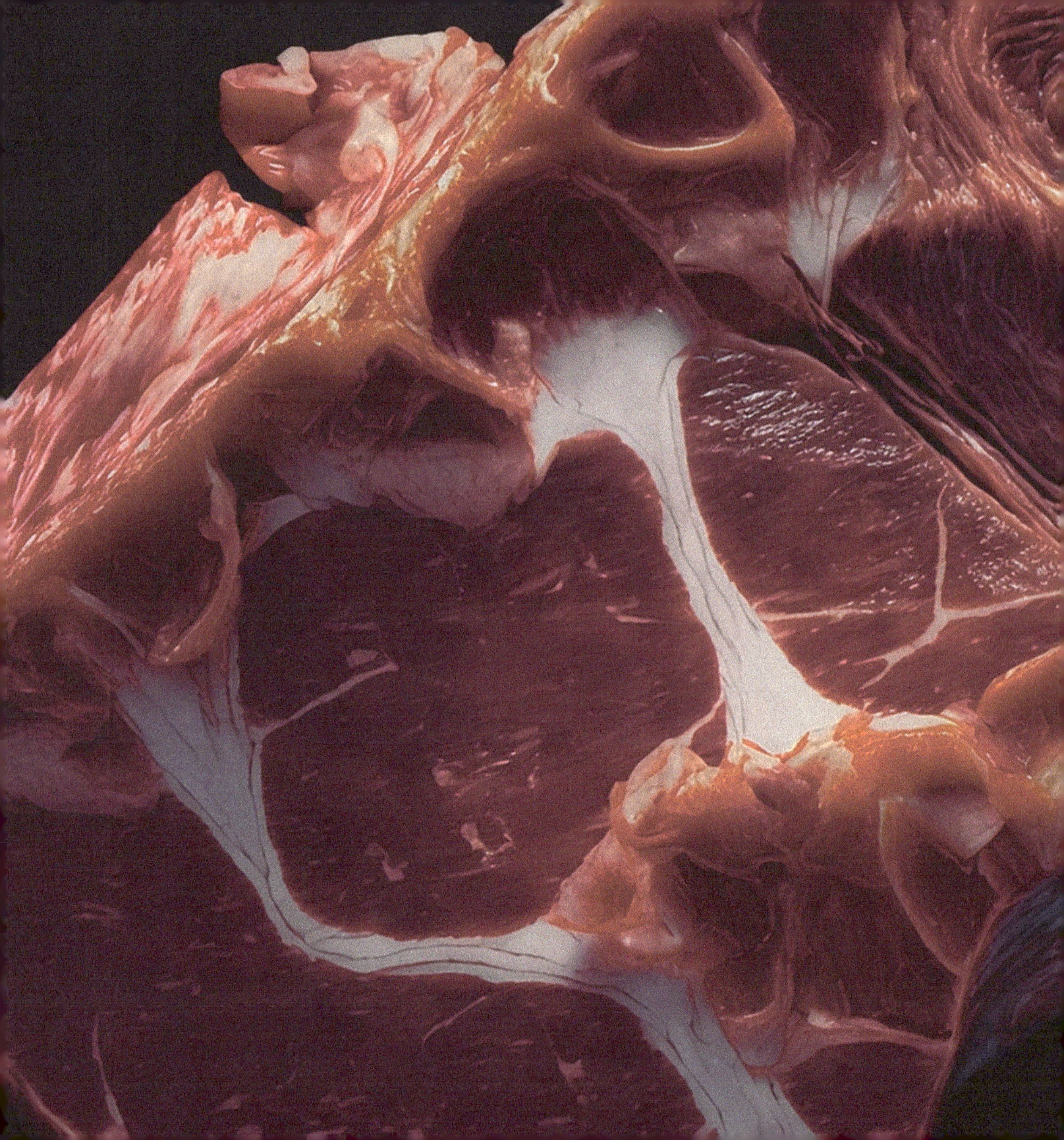

FLESH

A noun that refers to the soft substance that covers the bones of a human or animal body. In a general sense, *"flesh"* can also be used to refer to the physical body in general. *"Flesh"* appears in many idioms, such as *"a pound of flesh"* (something owed and difficult to provide); *"press the flesh"* (shake hands, as on the campaign trail), and *"flesh out"* (to provide more information).

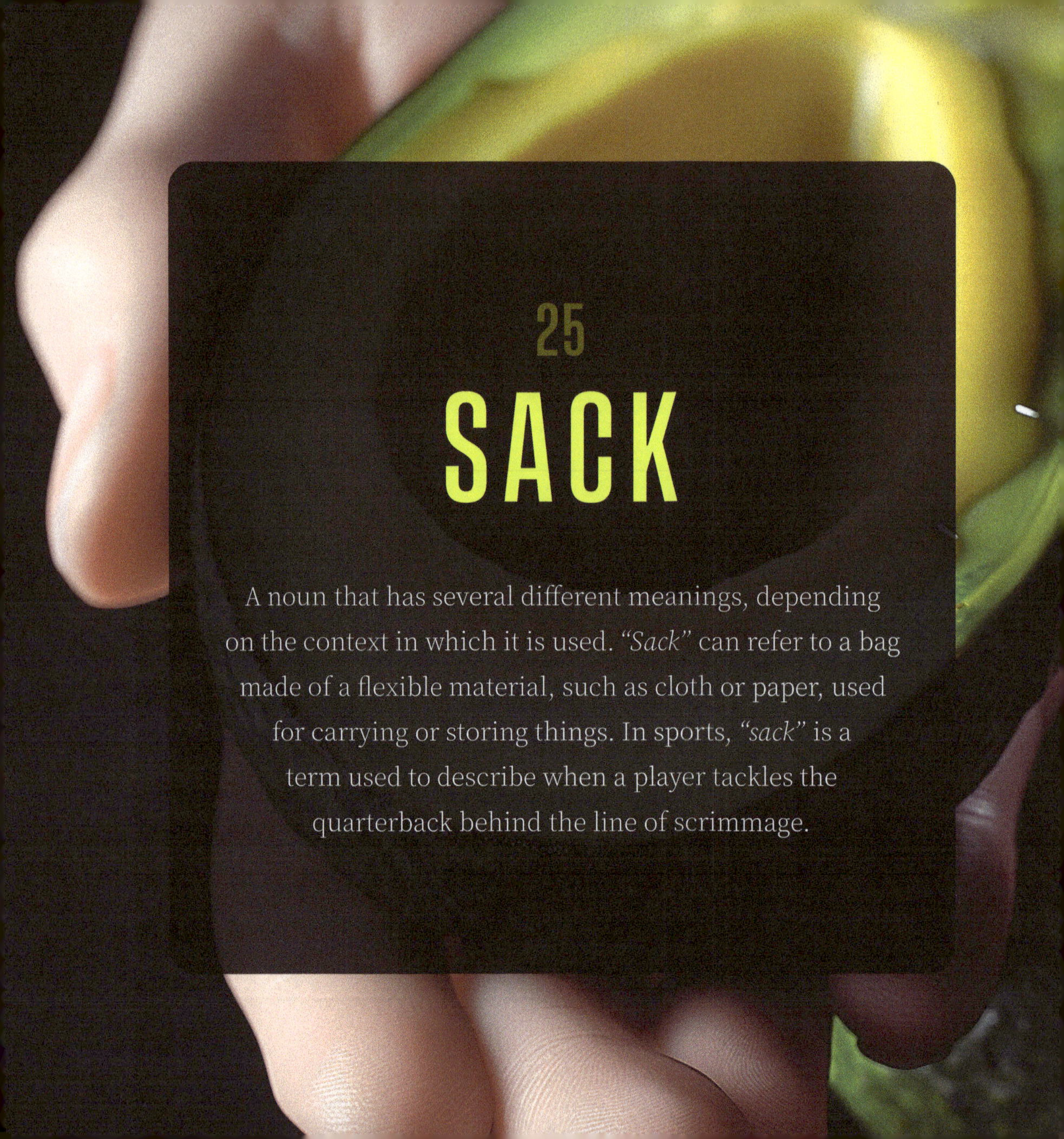

SACK

A noun that has several different meanings, depending on the context in which it is used. *"Sack"* can refer to a bag made of a flexible material, such as cloth or paper, used for carrying or storing things. In sports, *"sack"* is a term used to describe when a player tackles the quarterback behind the line of scrimmage.

PANTIES

Originally a shortened version of pantaloons or underpants, *"panties"* describes a type of undergarment that covers the lower body. Panties can be designed in a variety of styles, including briefs, thongs, and boy shorts, and are often used for both comfort and modesty.

THRUST

A verb that means to push or drive something forward
with force and is often used in aerodynamics. It can also refer
to a sudden movement in a particular direction. For example,
you might thrust a sword into someone, or you might
thrust your way through a crowded room.

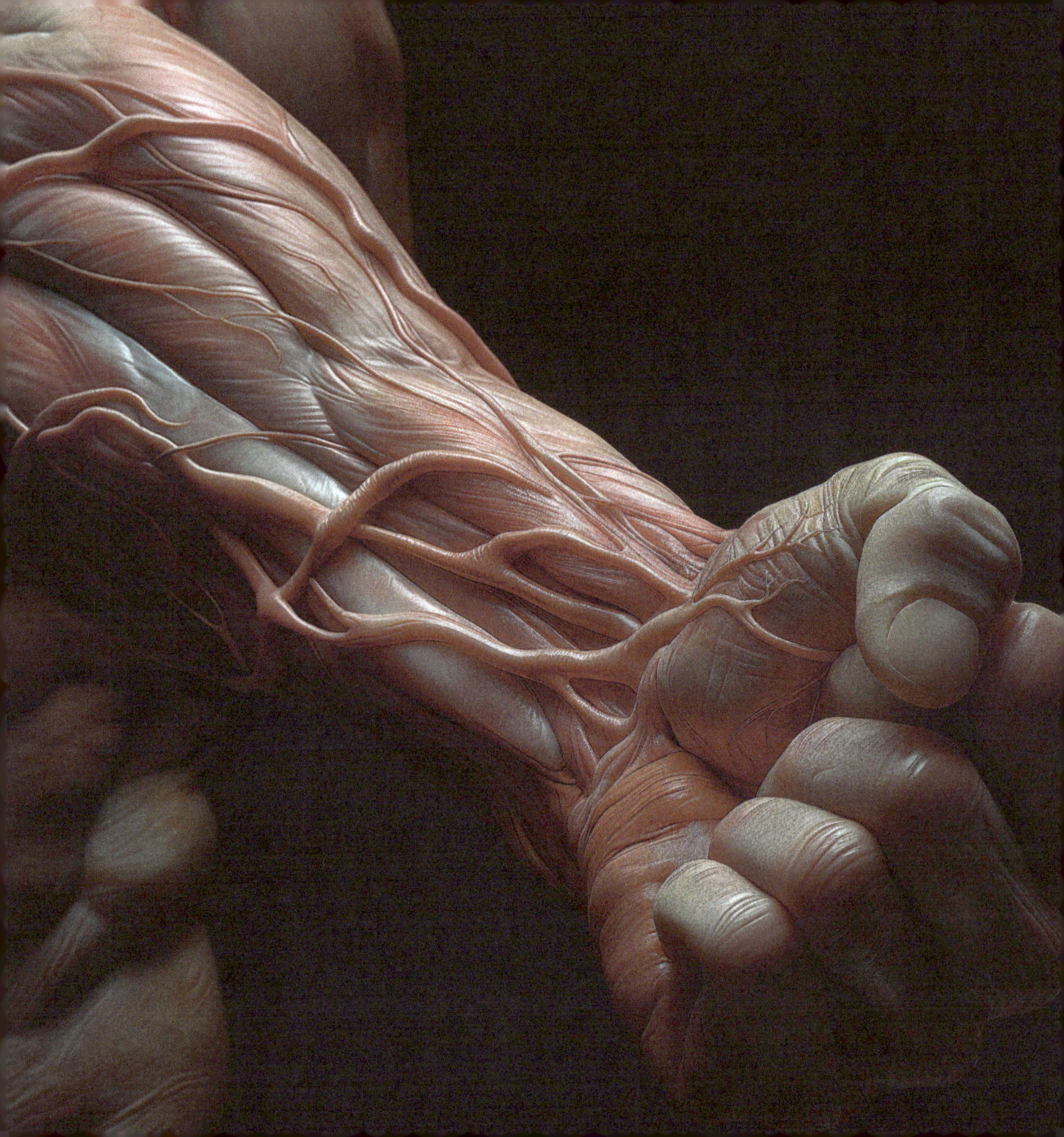

VEINY

An adjective used to describe something that has many visible veins. This can refer to the appearance of skin, leaves, or any other object that has a network of veins running through it.

CRUSTY

An adjective used to describe something that is
covered in a hard or brittle layer, often dried and encrusted.
This can refer to old food, old skin, or any other object that has
a tough outer layer that is difficult to remove. It's also a
derogatory term to describe an old, irritable person,
as in *"a crusty grandfather."*

30

SQUIRT

A verb referring to the sudden act of emitting a
small amount of liquid. In slang, it's a noun describing
a person who is insignificant and possibly annoying.

STOOL

A noun used to describe a type of furniture, such as
a seat or a footstool. It can also be used to describe solid
waste that is eliminated from the body.

STROKE

As a verb, *"to stroke"* means to move a hand or an object gently along a surface or through something, usually in a caressing or soothing manner. In a sexual context, "stroke" can be used as a slang term to refer to manual stimulation or touch.

BUSH

A noun that refers to various things including
a dense group of shrubs, a small group of trees, or an
area of dense vegetation. Also commonly referred to
as male and/or female pubic genital hair.

DRY ROT

An adjective that refers to a type of wood decay caused
by certain fungi, resulting in the wood becoming dry and
brittle, often with a characteristic musty odor.

35

SOIL

A noun referring to the top layer of earth that
is composed of organic and inorganic materials,
including decomposed plants and animals, as well
as rock fragments. When used as a verb it
can refer to dirtying one's pants.

PUMP

A verb that refers to various actions such as forcing fluid
or air into or out of something, moving something with a repeating
motion, or operating a machine with a similar action. It can
also refer to how someone feels after lifting lots of weights
and their muscles are engorged.

37

UNIT

As a noun, *"unit"* can refer to various things,
including a single item or entity, a measuring device,
a system or machine, or a military organization.

CREAM

As a noun, cream is the fatty liquid which rises to the top of milk and is used in cooking or as an accompaniment to desserts. It can also be a thick liquid applied to treat and soften the skin. The word "cream" can also be used as a slang term to refer to sexual arousal or ejaculation, as in the phrase "cream his / her pants."

MIDJOURNEY AI OUTTAKES

DEDICATION

This book is a tribute to that initial group of colleagues *(you know who you are)* who took a strategic planning session and drove it off course, turning it into something totally unrelated, fun, and very memorable.

THANK YOU

I want to thank my family, friends, and colleagues
who have encouraged me to take a spark of an idea and run
with it. Thanks for the many laughs as we built a list of words
that has now become the *Book of those words*™.

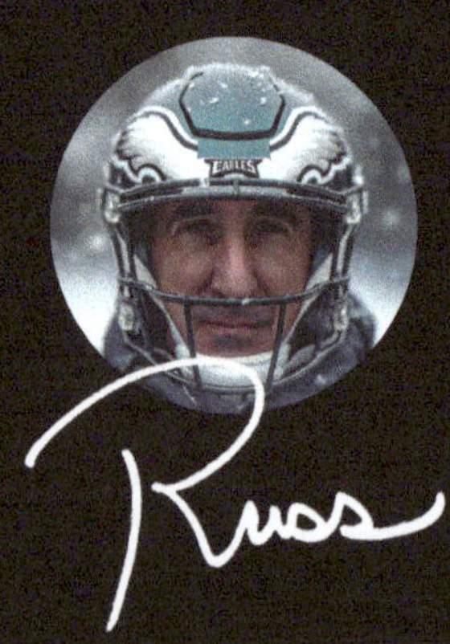

A special thank you to Janice Bissell, Andrew Bogucki, Sarah Bowen, David Garcia, Renee Malfi, and Annick Wydooghe, and to anyone I may have missed who contributed to this book.

A very special thank you to my business partners, Michael McDonald and Zave Smith. Michael, Xhilarate's Creative Director, spent endless hours learning and mastering Midjourney AI®, the AI program from which the cover-to-cover visuals were created. It is through his creative passion and unwavering desire to master something new, that my vision for this book became a reality. Zave Smith, Xhilarate's Chief Inspiration Officer, provided insight for the visuals and plenty of off-color commentary to keep us laughing throughout the process.

Thank you to Darcy Grabenstein whose mastery of words took what ChatGPT® provided, editing and organizing it into content reflective of the human language.

For Beth, B.J., and Elizabeth (aka Betsy)